THE
COST
OF
MONEY

A PRAGMATIC INSIGHT INTO THE
NIGERIAN HOUSING MARKET

Nelson N. Elemi

The Cost of Money

Copyright © 2021 by Nelson N. Elemi

ISBN: 9798475834770

All rights reserved.

No part of this publication may be reproduced, stored or transmitted in any form or by any means, electronic, mechanical, photocopying, recording, scanning, or otherwise without written permission from the publisher. It is illegal to copy this book, post it to a website, or distribute it by any other means without permission.

Printed in the United States of America

To the tribe, for all your encouragement and support…I will always be grateful.

Preface

I apologize to readers of this book for the delivery methodology used. During the editing stage, my editors were concerned about how short the work is and how quickly ideas discussed; are breezed over without in-depth explanations.

It has come to my attention that I seem to be an overly optimistic person and drawn to lost causes, with an unhealthy appetite for uphill battles. In my business life, the most tasking prospects seem to attract me the most, with lots of late nights invested into solving problems that probably should be avoided.

In writing this book, I intend to start a conversation, one that should be had more often with a readiness to take steps that can potentially reduce the list of uphill battles that my compulsions very often endear me to, hopefully.

CONTENT

Preface ii

The Deficit Myth 1

Supply Problem 21

Money Problem 34

Big Pond Mindset 45

The Elephant in the Room 58

The Social Deficit 76

Forward unto Dawn 88

The Deficit Myth

The first lesson of economics is scarcity: There is never enough of anything to satisfy all those who want it. The first lesson of politics is to disregard the first lesson of economics
Thomas Sowell

The moment any rational individual gets any meaningful exposure to the Nigerian housing market, it starts to question a handful of so-called facts. Facts like Nigeria's 17 million housing deficit that's often publicizing; very quickly, that figure begins to look overly unreliable and lose its validity once substantially critiqued. In all honesty, whenever we publish or talk about economic numbers in Nigeria.

I have very little faith in given details by ostensible professionals that reverberate numbers that **cannot** be validated or verified by any meaningful data.

> "When you want to help people, you tell them the truth. When you want to help yourself, you tell them what they want to hear."

By their definition, a housing deficit or shortage is when housing production falls behind demand. According to Thomas Sowell, "when you want to help people, you tell them the truth. When you want to help yourself, you tell them what they want to hear". It doesn't take an overly imaginative mind to know where this is going.

For Nigeria to claim it has a housing deficit problem; is ridiculous and should be challenged by all that operate in this sector. We have a poverty issue, not a housing deficit issue.

> For Nigeria to claim it has a housing deficit problem is ridiculous and should be challenged by all that operate in this sector. We have a poverty issue, not a housing deficit issue.

Nigeria's housing market is often mischaracterized as existential. As a dire social inadequacy that can slowly morph into a cataclysmic event of monumental proportions, which has the potential to trigger social unrest. But the reality is somewhat more complicated than we often like to admit. While comparing the average number of individuals to the estimated number of houses in the country (which more comprehensive data is required), you might get a higher percentage when compared to other countries.

This higher dependence is predominantly a factor of social structure, cultural norms, and an extremely high dependence ratio, which has very little to do with unsatisfied demand.

> ...it is still common to see adults in their late thirties living with their parents; this is mostly a product of factors like culture, late entry into the labour market, underemployment, high costs of rent and ineffective mortgage financial services

Anyone that actually understands Nigeria knows that there is a difference in demographic structure between rural areas and urban centers.

Also, regional cultural considerations and trends have to be examined and put into context when analyzing details about the housing market. Nigeria is often oversimplified and by lazy generalizations, which are wildly misleading at best and mostly incomplete.

It is still common to see adults in their late thirties living with their parents; this is partly a product of factors like culture, late entry into the labor market, underemployment (inability of wages to keep up with inflation), and ineffective mortgage financial services.

There is a significant and problematic lag in the period of entry by Nigerians into the housing market, with a youth unemployment rate projected to be as high as 32 percent (excluding massive underemployment). Paradoxically, after years of government-sponsored housing programs and subsidized public mortgage services, it is still commonplace to see individuals in the public sector build their first home at the end of their careers using bulk entitlements.

Others in the private sector rely on expensive loans or salary advances to facilitate the home-building process. Another fact that we can't overlook is that it's common for individuals to priorities building in their ancestral home (village) first before focusing on owning a home in their primary place of residence.

> …youth unemployment and underemployment is the largest single contributor to an exceptionally high dependence culture, which significantly cripples their ability to either rent or buy homes at a younger age.

This is something our well-meaning analysts have failed to explore, as rural developments usually lack any attention or interest from mortgage service providers and are characterized by out-of-pocket expenditure. The market balance between home-ownership and affordable rental housing is an important aspect, which should be properly analyzed by policy-makers.

…enormous misdirection by industry expects has caused a trend of unrelenting speculative investment in the housing market that has only further created the issue of excess supply especially in major cities

A pragmatic outline on rural and urban housing policies should be mapped up to suit the actual market demand instead of playing around with machinations aimed at justifying largescale housing works projects. In my experience, youth unemployment and underemployment is the largest single contributor to an exceptionally high dependence culture, which significantly cripples their ability to either rent or buy homes at a younger age. This is where a homeownership-centered policy can be problematic as it does not pay attention to affordable rental housing for the younger generation, those with limited earnings, or individuals that require the flexibility that renting affords.

In my experience, youth unemployment and underemployment is the largest single contributor to an exceptionally high dependence culture, which significantly cripples the youth's ability to either rent or buy homes at a younger age.

This is where a homeownership-centered policy can be problematic as it does not pay attention to affordable rental housing for the younger generation, those with limited earnings, or individuals that require the flexibility that renting affords.

> ...a more sustainable approach by the public sector in providing affordable housing will be in the form of policies that encourage or ensure the reduction of the

cost mortgage loan and the cost of commercial lending for affordable housing real estate development.

However, whenever the conversation about the housing deficit comes up, you always hear so-called industry experts talk about the need for more direct government intervention with an increase in the number of enormously problematic social housing projects around the country.

This is where I disagree completely; from my observations, largescale public low-cost housing projects in Nigeria are usually disastrous as there fail to provide the adequate necessities required to tackle a housing deficit.

From my experience, a more sustainable approach by the public sector in providing affordable housing will be in the form of policies that encourage or ensure the reduction of the cost of a mortgage loan and the cost of commercial lending for affordable housing real estate development. Also, more public-sponsored research is required for the development and eventual application of localized building technology. Understanding demographic traits and appreciating divergent aspects of the housing market is imperative to properly outlining any comprehensive data about the housing market. Otherwise, making blanket assumptions and incorrect generalizations creates a wildly speculative investment culture.

This enormous misdirection by industry expects has caused a trend of unrelenting speculative investment in the housing market that has only further created the issue of excess supply or mismatched supply, especially in major cities.

> ...the major deficit that exists today in the housing market is an incentive for investors to make long-term commitments, diversity of supply, the capacity of demand, and sustainability in development.

Even with the normalcy of massive empty estates with similarities to ghost cities in China, some still argue that this is caused by a mismatch between the capacity of demand

and available supply and a need to build cheaper with public funds.

This kind of mindset discourages investment in affordable housing projects which by most indicators is the most underserved aspect of the market and requires more private participation.
The issue of subsidized or public housing is a topic that is still heavily debated to this day in most developed or advanced economies. With some very credible arguments on both sides; like all things in life invariably do.

However, in each isolated scenario, there is a need to not misdiagnose the market and implement policies that become catastrophic with long-term economic, social, and environmental consequences.

From my observation, some social housing projects do have significant positives but this is a policy that should be designed with a clear understanding of its target beneficiaries and not misconstrued as a way to solve a housing deficit.

> …some social housing projects do have significant positives but this is a policy that should be designed with a clear understanding of its target beneficiaries and not misconstrued as a way to solve a housing deficit.

With a lot of developed countries still trying to design a balanced policy for housing accessibility, Nigeria prioritizes homeownership over affordable rental housing which limits the functionality of the housing market as a whole.

Nigeria's approach towards affordable homeownership in the context of subsidized long-term mortgages has recorded mixed successes, especially in its implementation. Access to this service is still limited and is yet to make a significant impact across the country. The policy in itself is effective and has recorded massive success, but is still limited in its availability, execution, scope and doesn't necessarily assist developers in escaping the high cost of capital.

Policymakers at all levels still have a long way to go in designing and implementing a progressive mindset as the major deficit that exists today in the housing market is an incentive for investors to make long-term commitments, diversity of supply, the capacity of demand, and sustainability in development.

Looking at the market from a micro or localized perspective is necessary, as it guides policymakers, investors, and other specialists in understanding the market better. Blatant oversimplification is somewhat reminiscent of imperialism and does not reflect the intent of society to maximize its potential.

In a globalized world, it is often easy to get mislead with terms like free trade and lose sight of the fact that business imperialism persists in more ways than we like to admit.

> …localized potential is destroyed or mostly neglected to create extractable value which

> subsequently limits economic growth and diversification.

This is often catastrophic, as localized potential is destroyed or mostly neglected to create extractable value which subsequently limits economic growth and diversification. This form of centralist mindset is what often creates simplified narratives of aspects of our housing market that are misleading.
I believe the housing market has a lot of potential for growth in certain locations, but the required approach to exploring this potential is generally misunderstood. Much study is required with an adequate framework designed at a local level with support from state and federal sponsored programs.

> Climatic conditions, geopolitics and economic opportunities will play decisive roles in what drives the housing market.

As Nigeria urbanizes, they will be an increase in demand for new homes and certain areas will experience exponential growth, others will not. Others might even experience a decline. Climatic conditions, geopolitics, and economic opportunities will play decisive roles in what drives the housing market.

Therefore, understanding what is required is imperative, and the first step involves having valid data that can be objectively analyzed with increased collaboration between all stakeholders in the private and public sectors. It consequently is the responsibility of local and state governments to actively design policies and housing framework that encourages responsible investment in the housing market.

Supply Problem

Competition is always a good thing. It forces us to do our best. A monopoly renders people complacent and satisfied with mediocrity.
Nancy Pearcey

Basic economics teaches us that once an essential commodity lacks close substitutes, its price increases, and in an economy plagued by constant inflation, this can ultimately become catastrophic.
Observing the demand elasticity of any commodity, it is necessary to understand competitive alternatives that can serve as substitutes in the event of a price increase.

...when exploring aspects of the housing market that contribute significantly to an unsustainable

> cost of construction, it became obvious that our overreliance on cement as a core building material plays a pivotal role.

This is why every single country on earth has some form of antitrust law to protect its citizens from predatory business practices while ensuring fair competition. Bid rigging, price-fixing, market allocation, and any form of business monopoly are bad for a country and ultimately disastrous for consumers.

Therefore, when exploring aspects of the housing market that contribute significantly to an unsustainable cost of construction, it became obvious that our overreliance on cement and concrete blocks as a core building material plays a pivotal role.

Concrete is incredibly reliable and integral to Nigeria because it delivers cost-effectively, with an incredibly low carbon footprint over its lifecycle with longevity and resilience. About 10 billion tons of concrete are produced each year, making it the most consumed substance on earth, second only to water.

It is used worldwide in different formats for home construction with varying degrees of success and application. Over 70% of the world's population lives in some form of a concrete structure due to its durability and strength. However, our usage of cement in Nigeria is overly streamlined and somewhat uniform in application across the entire country.

This has created a market monopoly with dire consequences and an unrivaled demand extremely limited in scope.

> ...our usage of cement in Nigeria is overly streamlined and somewhat uniform in application across the entire country.

This has created a market monopoly with dire consequences and an unrivaled demand that is extremely limited in scope. Given this, a conversation I often have with developers and real estate investors about the need for market reform and diversification in delivery.

In my opinion, this is probably one of the very few issues that can be entirely tackled by the private sector.

I do not generally believe in advocating for any particular building method or technology, nor do I intend to. But I believe that having an open market with available choices will create a more competitive localized market for building materials.

> The potential for localized solutions are endless and requires more support from the demand and supply side of the market.

A healthy housing market scenario will have varied building materials; from concrete blocks to composite formwork, or cross-laminated timber (CLT). The potential for localized solutions is endless and requires more support from the demand and supply side of the market. If Nigeria had a housing market that had the support of government regulators and financial institutions.

> There's a need to educate aspiring homeowners and builders about diverse building methods, technologies, and materials that have the potential to revolutionize the housing market in terms of cost, quality, sustainability, and speed of delivery.

Including the acceptability of prospective builders or homeowners, price elasticity will ensure the emergence of healthy competition. With a diverse number of natural resources that have multiple industrial applications with domestic and foreign potential utilization in construction.

There's a need to educate aspiring homeowners and builders about other building methods, technologies, and materials that have the potential to revolutionize the housing market in terms of cost, quality, sustainability, and speed of delivery.

> Widespread adoption will need to be achieved to ensure critical mass in the diversification of this sector with consumer's tastes and confidence open to new ideas.

So far cement has been significantly explored with successes recorded in this sector. However, more is required in the cement industry to ensure that they adopt and apply new technologies that help to reduce their CO2 emissions from industrial and energy activities.

> …substandard homes can also be tackled; as from my personal experience, a lot of developers end up building low-quality homes due to high/increasing prices of building materials and are forced to cut corners just to make a profit.

Cement has become the single most important commodity in home construction as it has become the base material for about 98% of new homes built in Nigeria today.

Uniquely, this universality is also endemic in the method to which it is applied, which subsequently gives rise to a constant increase in the cost of construction. The case for cement is understandable as it's one of the few materials that Nigeria has successfully explored by both local and international corporations.

But here's something we've entirely missed; the cost for building new homes can be reduced significantly if developers create new demand for other locally sourced materials like polystyrene (from our abundant oil reserves), cross-laminated timber (CLT), and other composite materials.

This can be explored to create a diversity of choice and healthy competition to reduce the eventual cost of homes construction.

Widespread adoption will need to be achieved to ensure critical mass in the diversification of this sector with consumer's tastes and confidence open to new ideas. Developers/builders have a role to play in achieving this by educating prospective clients on the availability of choices and invariably benefit the most from having a competitive market of quality options to choose from. It is a win-win situation; the price of homes stabilizes over time, and developers can improve their profit margins without necessarily reducing quality.

The case of substandard homes can also be tackled. From my personal experience, a large number of developers end up building low-quality homes due to high/increasing prices of building materials and are forced to cut corners just to make a profit.

> ...due to changing taste and inflation, very few developers still operate in this space with more focus and investment in the luxury market as it guarantees healthier profit margins and price flexibility.

In reality, few developers set out to build substandard properties (apart from the truly dishonest ones), especially if they have any intention of growing in the real estate sector. But overly streamlined supply and constant inflation create difficulties for those operating in the housing market, especially the developers.

I know builders that have given up on building homes or left the country entirely because they can't keep up with a continuously drifting landscape. Most focus solely on building luxury or tagging their projects as luxurious. This is because, with so-called high-end real estate, value is purely subjective.

When I got into real estate in 2014, there was a trend in the market of providing affordable housing for the growing middle class. Fast-forward to 2021, due to rapid inflation, very few developers still operate in this space with more focus and investment in the luxury market as it guarantees healthier profit margins and price flexibility.

For the cost of building new homes to become more affordable, commitments will be required in the form of research and development grants for localized solutions that can be scaled up and adequately implemented. This diversification will eventually help in fostering a competitive market and ensure the availability of supply and much-needed employment in the industrial sector.

> investments will have to be made into R&D of localized solutions that can be scaled up which will eventually help to create healthy competition in the availability of supply and much-needed employment in the industrial sector.

There is a need for the public and financial sector to incentivize developers and home builders to adopt proven localized alternatives, with the capacity to reduce overall the cost of construction.

Money Problem

Money is not everything, but is probably second to Oxygen.
Manoj Arora

I am a prodigious consumer of all sorts of information; eBooks, Podcasts, YouTube, Wikipedia, some might even call me an information junkie. Constantly assimilating new data and spilling unsolicited information as casual conversations. In my normal unbearable way, after watching a piece on The Economist titled 'How an obsession with homeownership can ruin the economy. I could not help but share this new information I had, like a kid with a new toy, to my business partner and best mate, Stanley.

An aspect of the video explored the renting culture between Switzerland and the UK; a woman in Switzerland, found out that her reference interest on her rented apartment had reduced. She then wrote to her landlord requesting for her rent to also be reduced. And within 3 months, her landlord honored her request.

the distinctive comparison between rent and homeownership, economists are yet to conclusively make a valid claim on which has a better economic and social significance to the individual and economy or what equates to a healthy balance.

I could immediately see the shock and disbelief on his face, "I have never heard of rent dropping because a tenant asked" he said, my guy had to watch the video himself. When making the distinctive comparison between rent and homeownership, economists are yet to conclusively make a valid claim on which has a better economic and social significance to the individual and economy or what equates to a healthy balance.

This comparison however, is a great way to observe how the *cost of money* can affect a market and consumer behavior irrespective of the government policy.

Therefore, as a lifelong student of social development economics with an obsession with positive micro outcomes in any planning scenario, I usually propose decisions that significantly improve the individual (family) circumstances over time. Also, my work over the years evolves around understanding the desires, concerns, and financial disposition of individuals and how it affects their attitude towards homeownership.

For this reason, I try to understand individual factors that affect the eventual choices made, especially factors that can be defined as externalities; usually the cost of capital.

> ...I noticed a desire for homeownership amongst a significant chunk of the population, triggered by a handful of key contributing factors; economic uncertainly, constant inflation, and an overall

feeling of not getting value for money on a rented property

Nigeria has a money problem that most economists have failed to properly write or discuss extensively. We usually assume that everybody understands the mechanics of inflation, exchange, and interest rate. Most prospective homeowners and renters are unaware of the role that the cost of money plays in creating access to affordable housing.

Understanding how all these affect individual sectors is imperative, especially one as fundamental as housing. In the modern world, demand and supply are significantly affected by these economic factors. However, factors like tradition or culture serve as secondary indicators of prevailing trends.

In exploring the cost of money in housing trends, I noticed a desire for homeownership (not necessarily demand) amongst a significant section of the population. This trend is mostly due to a handful of key contributing factors: economic uncertainly, constant inflation, and an overall feeling of not getting value for money on a rented property.

From my experience, value for money is probably one of the most significant contributors to this problem. It has created a culture amongst the urban population of constantly obsessing about homeownership which contributes to a misdiagnosed case of excess demand subsequently destabilizes prices across the entire housing market.

> ...most Nigerians aspire to own homes not as an investment decision but as a safeguard against uncertain times...this anxiety is significantly reduced with a different approach to financing commercial real estate...

In my experience, most Nigerians aspire to own homes not as an investment decision but as a safeguard against uncertain times.

This anxiety is significantly reduced, with a different approach to financing commercial real estate, which consequentially reduces the cost of rent and the financial burden of the landlord.

Whenever affordable housing is explored, more attention should be paid to the potential positives of affordable renting. Including pragmatic steps to make it more accessible for middle to low-income earners while also financially viable for investors and builders.

> ...the banking sector has a lot to do in this area as it holds the key to providing flexible financing for affordable commercial development.

I feel the banking sector has a lot to do in this area as it holds the key to providing flexible financing for affordable commercial development.

In a scenario where a developer builds a rental property with 100% equity, there's usually a need for that property to recover said investment within a short period. Invariably, this puts that burden on renters in the form of high rent. However, if a developer puts down 10 or 20 percent equity on that same property with the rest financed by a bank at a reasonable rate, let's say 25 years. The landlord can afford a little bit of flexibility when fixing rent prices.

In countries with rent control laws, they have even gone a step further by mandating landlords by law; to keep their rent as close as possible to their reference interest to ensure that renters are getting a fair deal and there is no exploitation.

Of course, this level of government involvement comes with a certain level of criticism. The jury is still out on the eventual outcome of this level of rent control and renter's protection. In my opinion, I feel a conversation about affordable housing can't be had without talking about affordable rental housing, as a one-sided focus on homeownership can be disastrous for the Nigerian economy. Without recourse, this can hamper the social mobility of the younger generation's desire for the flexibility of being able to move to urban centers for economic opportunities.

Also, the *cost of money* has to be addressed on an institutional level by both the public sector and the private sector. Only then can we meaningfully build homes that serve the market in a way that creates harmony in affordability for investors, builders, and prospective homeowners.

Big Pond Mindset

The single story creates stereotypes, and the problem with stereotypes is not that they are untrue, but that they are incomplete. They make one story become the only story.
Chimamanda Ngozi Adichie

Globalization is a unique phenomenon with consequences that can be rationalized as positives and negatives depending on perspective. This is a peculiar thing, especially when looking for opportunities in our extremely interconnected world. Unique risks, challenges, diversity of ideas, values, and culture can sometimes be overlooked.

When an investor or developer first enters the housing market, perspective is crucial. Nigeria has a wide range of opportunities in the real estate market, from massive commercial developments to boutique short-let properties. Opportunities are endless but also unique to certain locations, demography, and exciting policy.

> There's a need to have a clear understanding about where there's already existing demand, potential demand, and what's needed to develop said potential.

It is imperative to have a clear understanding of where there's already existing demand, potential demand, and what's needed to develop said potential. Some of the sub-sectors of the real estate market in Nigeria with explosive growth (e.g. short-let apartments) are areas where most experts previously did not see much potential. Discernment about what inspires trends in parts of the country is salient to both policymakers and investors. Quite often, causal indicators should be extensively researched and analysed to understand definite eventualities; positive or negative.

When exploring real estate investment opportunities in Nigeria, it's imperative to understand Nigeria as a whole, cultural/social trends, and political machinations. Whenever we approach the housing market in Africa or Nigeria, we are often guilty of lazy generalization and oversimplifying unique traits. We tend to look at the market from the perspective of what can best be described as a one-city approach and apply that same idea to sub-Saharan Africa.

My way of looking at the housing market in Nigeria is this: whichever city I intend to carry out a project, I apply the mindset of big fish in a small pond.

I try to understand the market and its uniqueness for what it is. Approaching the market this way is often decisive in understanding where demand for a particular investment exists or not. It also helps in building a roadmap for cultivating potential in areas that might seem uninviting.

Nigeria poses multiple risks for investors, with each geopolitical region having its characteristics and specific cities having their trends. This diversity in trait tends to perplex investors as certain kinds of housing projects do not have universal acceptability or have the same expected percentage of success.

> ...Nigeria as a whole should never be oversimplified by investors and most be viewed as a collection of small ponds instead of one giant pond with universal characteristics.

Nigeria has a healthy housing market, but as a whole, should never be oversimplified by investors. But must be viewed as a collection of small ponds instead of one giant pond with universal characteristics.

This mindset of simplification is a bi-product of business imperialism and a centralist perspective that is problematic for the country as most developers and mortgage institutions cluster themselves in Abuja and Lagos, constantly competing for scraps, unable to explore and develop the market elsewhere.

This is a criticism that I also have about the PMI's, which only set up offices in Abuja and Lagos. The majority of the country does not have adequate access to mortgage finance at the same level that the commercial banks provide.

A lot needs to be done by both policymakers and regulatory bodies to ensure proper distribution of these services across the country, either with direct physical availability or advantage of technology to provide access to all parts of the country.

I usually do project tours once a year to different parts of the country to explore investment opportunities in the housing market and other areas of interest. It is fascinating how very few individuals know about the FHS, its services, and how they can take advantage of it (especially those in the private sector).

Even public employees lack adequate understanding of their mortgage entitlements and only get to minuscule details when and if a developer informs them about it, which shouldn't be the case.

> ...the developer should have very little to do with educating clients about mortgage financing, this should be done by the

> professionals whose job it is to do so.

Ideally, the developer should have very little to do with educating clients about mortgage financing, which should remain the sole responsibility of the professionals whose job it is to do so.

In my experience, the best financial services are usually bespoke offers that are tailored to suit the specific location and need. The financial regulators should give state outfits certain flexibility to design mortgage requirements/ modalities based on their service area's unique characteristics.

> Once there's a competition for the certification of lands in Nigeria, the state governments

> will have to do more to certify land purchases or lose valuable revenue to the federal government.

This is because political machinations and state government policies very often impede the ability of individuals in those states to access housing opportunities. A typical example is where; governors do not certify land purchases or make provisions/delegate authority in their state, which further worsens housing inequality and creates unique challenges for investors.

One scenario that a lot of developers feel might force the hand of state governments to sit up is if the federal government set up a dedicated national directory where all land purchases in the states can be certified which takes the monopoly of the states to issue title on land purchases. Once there's a competition for the certification of lands in Nigeria, the state governments will have to do more to certify land purchases or lose valuable revenue to the federal government.

My suggestion is highly controversial. I believe a review and possible amendment by the federal legislature of the Land Use Act of 1978 (which in my opinion is terribly flawed and negatively contributes immensely to the economic prosperity of the country).

Another suggestion that should be explored is, to further incentivize banks to lend more to low or middle-income earners; by providing a legal, constitutional and regulatory framework for mortgage securities to be tradable. This will enable the

Federal Mortgage Bank to buy mortgages from banks after it is issued, at a feasible stipulated timeframe.

> This improves the market flexibility and liquidity which enables the banks to provide wider coverage for homeowners across multiple spectrums of the housing market.

It will significantly reduce risk and the long-term exposures that most banks tend to avoid. In turn, it will reduce the lifetime cost of a home mortgage as the FMB rates can be friendlier to homeowners. This form of refinancing, if made mainstream, can subsequently instigate much greater access to mortgage financing.

Mortgage securities are already tradable securities in most developed economies, including the USA. Entities like Freddie Mac and Fannie Mae buy up low-interest mortgages from banks, which subsequently provide liquidity, stability, and affordability to the mortgage market. This improves the market flexibility and liquidity, which enables the banks to provide wider coverage for homeowners across multiple spectrums of the housing market.

Given these issues, it's safe to imply that; responsible diversification of intent needs to be actualized across multiple spectrums before any meaningful manifestation of market satisfaction can be realized in the housing sector.

Given these issues, it's safe to imply that; responsible diversification of intent needs to be actualized across multiple spectrums before any meaningful manifestation of market satisfaction can be realized in the housing sector. And the mindset of the public sector at the state and local level needs to be aligned with these challenges; by diversifying expectations across the entire market in a way that allows for meaningful localized growth and market satisfaction.

The Elephant in the Room

One can see from space how the human race has changed the Earth. Nearly all of the available land has been cleared of forest and is now used for agriculture or urban development. The polar icecaps are shrinking and the desert areas are increasing. At night, the Earth is no longer dark, but large areas are lit up. All of this is evidence that human exploitation of the planet is reaching a critical limit. But human demands and expectations are ever-increasing. We cannot continue to pollute the atmosphere, poison the ocean and exhaust the land. There isn't any more available.
Stephen Hawking

In 1911 Nigeria had a population of about 16 million. Today after a hundred and ten years, Nigeria has over 211 million inhabitants and a forecast projecting 400 million in 2050, overtaking the United States as the third most populous nation. It might sound exciting for all the optimists out there, projecting massive economic potential.

However, this unprecedented demographic shift might open Pandora's Box and unleash devastating consequences. Whenever we have this conversation around overpopulation, very few grasp the extent to which this phenomenon affects our daily lives.

> Nigeria's land mass is just under a million square kilometer with over sixty percent of the land experiencing severe desertification.

While analyzing our population issue, it is imperative to understand the significance availability of land for expansion or economic development. Nigeria's landmass is just under a million square kilometers, with as much as sixty percent of the land experiencing varied levels of desertification.

Anybody that pays any attention to the current rate of desertification in the Sahara will understand how dire the situation is. With the loss of livelihood, arable land, and a fast-growing population, it does not take a crystal ball to see where this trend leads.

There is an insurgency issue in Northern Nigeria, twined by a seismic increase in piracy across the gulf of guinea. These problems are mainly caused by environmental degradation, with desertification in the north and rampant oil spills in the Niger Delta region. Much-needed land for agriculture, freshwater for fishing, and other economic opportunities in these regions have been significantly degraded or polluted.

Currently, the gulf of guinea is a hotspot for maritime piracy, with about 97 percent of kidnapping in the world occurring in this region. With hundreds of seafarers in 2020 alone kidnapped, in what has become known as pirate-alley. It is emblematic of decades of lacklustre environmental response and an unprecedented population boom with a labor market and economic structure that cannot keep up.

My company recently acquired 5 hectares of land in Calabar for commercial development. When the land preparation began, I visited the site for inspection and realized it was a cassava farm.

Compensations were issued to the farmers, but I could not help but worry. For a country with a limited landmass; a more adequate framework for land utilization has not been properly implemented.

While I struggled to reconcile this very uncomfortable reality with the fact that my clients had made it clear that there required a 900 square meter land for their property. It made me disillusioned with the current state of things, and how more effort is needed from governments and the private sector in addressing the seriousness of this issue.

As our population grows and more resources are needed to provide food or essential raw materials for economic development, everybody needs to reevaluate certain beliefs about how land is used including unchecked expansion of our urban spaces.

> ...the way we grow food, transport people, build homes, generate and consume energy all contribute immensely to creating a primordial hellscape of existential proportions that no fairly honest person can ignore.

Nigeria is at the cusp of an environmental and demographic crisis, coupled with a seemingly ignorant approach to the growing inevitable.

> ...there have been constant clashes of cattle herders and farming communities in parts of Nigeria largely caused by

> environmental issues, but largely politicized as most things often do; with the true culprit left unchecked.

What can't be ignored, however, is the degree to which our environment has been degraded by human activities; the way we grow food, transport people, build homes, generate and consume energy. It all contributes immensely to creating a primordial hellscape of existential proportions that no fairly honest person can ignore.

In Nigeria, the effects are far-reaching and have had a catastrophic impact on communities with a level of violence that has continued to breed mayhem across the country.

> ...a lot more needs to be done by all parties to ensure more discussion around the environmental impact of urban development projects and the sustainability of what we build, the resources we use, and how energy is consumed by the homes we build.

In Nigeria, the effects are far-reaching and have had a catastrophic impact on communities with a level of violence that has continued to breed mayhem across the country.

With much of the Sahel region becoming unsustainable, there have been constant clashes of cattle herders and farming communities in parts of Nigeria. Caused by environmental factors but heavily politicized as most things often do with the actual culprit being left unchecked.

We often imagine ourselves as curators of our destiny; our actions should reflex the reality of our fragile existence with much care paid to the planet we call home. We need to quickly figure out how to sustainably house and provide for a country with an extremely young population and rapid urbanization.

In my experience, very little attention is given in regards to; sustainability in the real estate market. A lot more needs to be done by all parties to ensure more discussion around the environmental impact of urban development projects and the sustainability of what we build, the resources we use, and the energy consumed in our homes.

> …developing economies have the unique advantage to curate urban centers that are truly sustainable and contribute positively to the environment. In Nigeria, developers have the freedom to design and build projects with very little public regulation or oversight.

Developing economies have a unique advantage; to curate urban centers that are truly sustainable and contribute positively to the environment.

In Nigeria, developers have the freedom to design and build projects with extreme flexibility in terms of public regulation.

This has sometimes birth hideous monstrosities, but could potentially create a culture of creativity and sustainability. Which is necessitates the provision of all the necessary utilities that are lacking in our urban centers.

> There's a growing trend among developers to sell people luxury, when in reality what the market actually craves is diversity, affordability, sustainability and urbanization.

Additions like; sewage treatment, proper drainages, reliable clean energy, and soulful cohesive communities are lost to our urban dwellers with the inclusion of common areas.

There is a growing trend among developers to sell people luxury, in reality, what the market craves is diversity, affordability, sustainability, and urbanization. I believe it is the responsibility of those of means and resources to help curate a better future. To do so with a conscious effort to protect the environment and design projects that propel us into a future with less environmental pollution.

There's an opportunity to create a framework for future developments by the private sector in a way that democratizes the way urbanization is currently imagined in Nigeria, with increased collaboration city the public sector.

In 2021, we've seen widespread evidence of the effects of our warming climates, from extreme cases of heatwaves in parts of Asia and North America to massive flooding in Europe. Nigeria is not exempt from this as we see more southward migration in the country with continuous clashes by communities and nomadic tribes. A need for a more hands-on framework is necessary.

> It's my opinion that a more robust framework at the federal state and local level is mandated to ensure a more comprehensive land management plan for a more sustainable and efficient usage of land for housing developments.

The largest investments today in Nigeria remain the infrastructure for the expansion and development of the crude oil industry. However, the report from the 2021 Intergovernmental Panel on Climate Change (IPCC) paints a bleak picture of the future. I will try not to get into specific details, but it reaffirms what we are already experiencing - with more data to back the science.

In summary, our nearest future will be one filled with extreme weather events that will simply just become more recurrent. And requires governments around the world the invest in sectors that reduce the reliance on fossil fuel, environmental degradation, and deforestation. With the earn to decarbonize as soon as possible.

On the part of the private sector, the IPCC report should be a constant reminder that building a future that isn't future-proof is a bad investment. As more ecosystems get destroyed to create space for more housing developments in urban areas with population increase.

> However, as we slowly develop our urban spaces for a fast urbanizing society, there's a need to invest in cleaners sources of energy and construction materials that are more sustainable.

It's imperative, that a robust framework at the federal, state and local levels be drafted and effectively implemented. To ensure a more comprehensive land management plan; for more sustainable and efficient use of space for housing developments.

The construction industry is responsible for 39 percent of carbon emissions globally, out of which 28 percent is from energy consumption and 11 percent from construction material.

When exploring climate change and its effects, it's important to understand who the major polluters are and the little contribution countries like Nigeria contribute to the warming of our planet.

However, as we slowly develop our urban spaces for a growing young population, there's a need to invest in clean sources of energy and construction materials that are more sustainable.

> How we chose to accommodate this colossal demographic shift, is what will make the difference between a manageable crisis and an unmitigated catastrophe.

The financial sector needs to become a responsible partner in prioritizing projects that take into consideration the carbon footprint and eventual energy requirements of housing development.

Also, priority needs to be emphasized on diversifying the delivery and supply of homes with an intentional encouragement of alternative building solutions that can be more eco-friendly. This ultimately reduces the carbon footprint of our urban expansion, preserves biodiversity, and creates homes that are built to be more sustainable in the way energy is used and interact with their environment.

Given the rise of migration to Europe by Nigerians, we need to understand that a significant portion of these individuals migrating from rural areas end up in major cities. How we chose to accommodate this colossal demographic shift will make the difference between a manageable crisis and an unmitigated catastrophe.

The Social Deficit

Inflation destroys savings, impedes planning, and discourages investment. That means less productivity and a lower standard of living
Kevin Brady

My father turned 71 during the writing of this book, and I had the opportunity to have a conversation about the book and other economic issues peculiar to Nigeria.

During our talk, he mentioned something that I had heard countless times before, but for some strange reason, I saw it from a completely different light and provided a lot of insight for this chapter.

> …housing or affordable housing in Nigeria is arguably the most

> reliable store of value and a great way to ride the waves of inflation.

In 1991, my father, working as an administrator for the local government in Cross River State, received a car refurbishing allowance of N10,000 and took out N4,000 from that to buy 100 bags of cement which served as the first important step towards building his first home. Over the next couple of months, he and my mother (a trader and teacher at the time) made sacrifices but eventually built their first home.

Fast-forward to today, about 30 years from 1991, a bag of cement cost about N3, 400 and can only represent a single drop in a bucket on the road to any meaningful housing project.

Therefore, affordable housing in Nigeria is arguably the most reliable store of value and a great way to ride the waves of inflation.

> …affordable housing presents middle-income families with financial security over time, it has proven to be arguably the most reliable store of value in Nigeria today…ensuring that gains of the past endure no matter how bad inflation gets over time.

He further talked about how quickly things lose value and how other investments like bonds, shares, and even material acquisitions like cars hold little value over time.

It made me realize something that was always in front of me the entire time, but I could only see the macroeconomic importance. As much as affordable housing presents middle-income families with financial security over time, it has proven to be arguably the most reliable store of value in Nigeria today.
By ensuring that the gains of the past endure no matter how severe inflation gets over time.

It's also a great way to ensure social inclusiveness in our drive to urbanize, as affordable housing provides generations access to neighborhoods, cities, and regions with high economic potential.

If the 2021 riots, looting, violence in South Africa, and the same during the END SARS protests in Nigeria, is an indictment of our social failings as developing countries in Africa. We've done very little to provide social inclusivity and economic opportunities to our growing young population who have been ostracized from society altogether and are mostly relegated to shantytowns in the outskirts of our major cities.

> If your middle-income earners lose that access, it creates a massive social and economic problem in the drive for economic development as individuals need access

> to these urban centers to participate productively in all economic opportunities available to them.

Even families that ordinarily are regarded as middle income, can no longer afford to own homes in major cities in Nigeria.

In retrospect, families that were regarded as middle-class can no longer afford to own homes in major cities in Nigeria. If the middle-class lose access, it creates a massive social and economic problem in the drive for economic growth; individuals need access to these urban centers to participate productively to ensure social inclusion.

A family that has a home in Lagos, Abuja, Calabar, Kano, or Port Harcourt automatically provides their children with a massive springboard to participate socially and economically with access to the best opportunities available in the country.

According to population projections by the United Nations for 2020, about 43 percent of Nigeria's population is comprised of children 0 - 14 years, with 19 percent young adults 15 – 24 years. With the median age at about 18 and over 70 percent of the population under 30. Nigeria requires a lot of future-proofing with urban centers designed to suit the needs of a diverse population with tastes that are uniquely different from those of their parents.

There is a need for more dense urban spaces with common areas for recreation and socializing. The malls cannot provide this and have failed to provide a common ground in advanced economies; why do we expect it to succeed in Nigeria.

> With the median age at about 18 and over 70 percent of the population under 30, Nigeria requires a lot of future-proofing with urban centers designed to suit the needs of a diverse population with tastes and needs that are uniquely different from those of their parents.

There's a need for the country to focus heavily on affordable rental housing as the younger generation requires the flexibility of renting in areas with good educational facilities, economic opportunities, and social activities. Something that a lot of industry experts have failed to observe is that the emergence of short-let apartments, which has many investors; excited is a symptom of this problem.

We don't necessarily have a significant deficit of rental properties, as much as a shortage of dense urbanized affordable rental districts with common spaces that foster community.

> The growth of the very exciting short-let apartment niches, in reality, is actually caused by a shortage of quality affordable rental housing within the city…

> The public and banking sector also needs to realize that commercial real estate lending

> for affordable rental spaces is the most underserved area but also the part of the market that has the most potential for growth over the next coming years.

In reality, the growth of the exciting short-let apartment niches is the tenet of a shortage of quality affordable rental housing within major cities. Because, the majority of those that patronize short-let apartments in cities like Abuja, Lagos, and Calabar are already residents of those very same cities.

I believe more effort should be paid to this area by the government in their campaign for affordable housing as this reality keeps up with the numbers available in our demographic outlook.

> ...more inclusive planning and investment are done in making our urban centers more affordable and accessible by the growing population of youths in the country, this will potentially spur innovation and creativity which increases economic participation.

The banking sector also needs to realize that commercial real estate lending for affordable rental spaces is the most underserved sub-sector, and also part of the market that has the most potential for growth over the next coming years.

In my opinion, if more inclusive planning and investment are done in making our urban centers more affordable and accessible to the growing population of youths in the country, this will potentially spur innovation and creativity which increases economic participation.

Forward unto Dawn

A lie that can't be easily disproven by obviously facts, is one that once spoken; manifests its own reality, and thus becomes a self-fulfilling prophecy.
Anonymous

There is a saying in Puerto Rico that goes, "when the river sounds, it's because it brings water" this means that when everyone has the same complaint, there is a problem that needs fixing. This book is not intended to be some form of intellectual masterpiece or overly insightful, with cryptic details that are unknown to many.

It is a conversation starter; one that hopefully identifies significant indicators, norms, and challenges that hopefully kickstart the process of building a more pragmatic roadmap for society.

By most estimates, Nigeria's annual urbanization rate is slightly above 4 percent on average. It is indicative of a rural-urban migration that is common in developing nations as people leave the rural areas for higher wages and more economic opportunities in cities.

An example of this is the United States that experienced its urbanization during the late 19th and early 20th centuries. This demographic shift consequently drove innovation and industrialization in cities with significant growth in the real estate market as demand continued to increase steadily over long periods.

This rapid urbanization has the potential for vast economic growth and an equally fascinating catastrophe if mishandled. With this in mind, it's imperative that we responsibly invest resources in ensuring that our urban areas provide the level of social inclusion present in our rural communities. More effort is required, as most housing projects today are designed and built to serve the ultra-high to high-income earners, and at best, the upper-middle class, with the rest of the population relegated to their fate.

> In any society, affordable housing is immensely important on an economic level and an indicator of social development.

This situation is unsustainable for the government, developers, and a growing middle class that is slowly becoming alienated from economic activities: like owning a home or having access to affordable rental options; which is critical for a lot of fundamental social developmental factors.

Furthermore, it is important to note the significance of adequate provisions for an inclusive integration in our urban centers. As is evident in how this affects migration and economic participation in Nigeria today. When cities like Lagos, Abuja, Calabar or Kano become less habitable by individuals migrating from rural areas, or young adults coming into the labour force, it creates a sense of disillusion which triggers both legal and illegal migration in search for greener pastures (i.e. Europe's current migrant crisis).

By building a housing market that is extremely streamlined in supply and target audience, we have created a situation that will further worsen the economic divide, inspire resentment and stifle creativity. It is not reckless to imply that; at this very moment, our overreliance on a streamlined supply of building materials and an inadequate approach, has created a crisis that can best be described as existential.

If the recent surge is civil unrest around the country is any indicator of a worsening trend, it shows that we've hit critical mass and will require radical changes in the way we view housing and how it affect everything else.

Research from multiple countries across the globe shows that access to affordable housing or housing security contributes significantly to economic mobility while reducing social unrest and crime. Therefore, in building urban spaces that are welcoming to the middleclass and a housing market that is inclusive, our cities will serve as growth aggregators with innovation and enterprise naturally spawning from these ecosystems. Affordability is required in both the homeownership and rental markets, as this is the only path to sustainable growth and greater economic participation.

> ...the public and private sector needs to be worked out with more access to low interest loans for commercial housing developments and long-term

> mortgage facilities for prospective homeowners.

In any society, affordable housing is exceedingly salient at an economic level and is an important indicator of social development. It creates more inclusive communities and strengthens individual access to economic opportunities by providing a great store of value for homeowners while improving productive participation through the availability of affordable rental housing, especially for the growing young middle-class.

> …rapid urbanization has the potential for great economic growth and an equally fascinating catastrophe if handled incorrectly.

We must incentivize investors to invest capital in socially impactful projects. By ensuring practical exit strategies in the form of; mortgages for buyers or low-interest loans for rental properties that are affordable.

While also ensuring the protection of our environment with wholesale land management policies, robust public transportation, and sustainable clean energy. Furthermore, grants by both the public and private sectors will help encourage localized innovation by promoting the need for research and development of the construction industry.

This will also help to reduce our over-reliance on imported building materials, which in turn reduces the overall carbon footprint of home construction.

> ...grants by both the public sector and private sector will be helpful in encouraging localized innovation by promoting the need for research and development of the construction industry.

Our export potential will also improve as localized solutions are implemented, scaled, and become more competitive on the international market.

Subsequently, these industrial outputs will also create jobs, which triggers a multipliers effect by increasing disposable income, and then creates growth in other sectors. We must take advantage of available technology like; factory prefabricated homes, 3D printing whole buildings, or individual components.

The importance of this in the coming years is self-evident, as reducing waste and improving industrial efficiency becomes mainstream, creating more sustainable job opportunities.

> Private companies should also be encouraged to take the risk to invest in new ideas and technology that can be scaled to service the housing market.

Private companies should also be encouraged to take risks by investing in new ideas and technology; efficiently scaled to service the housing market. These will also help in achieving affordability as there will be more competition which drives costs down. Therefore it improves the overall profitability of the sector as a whole, which attracts more capital investment.

Understanding the demographic shift in Nigeria, necessitate adequate policies and responses that can provide incentives to satisfy market demand. In doing so, we have to collate and analyze valid data of indicative factors that drive these demographic shifts. This is an important step in actually diagnosing tentative details aspects of the Nigerian housing market that lacks satisfactory attention.

It is often said that "charity begins at home", in this context, it is imperative to understand the extent to which the home plays significant role in society.

It is imperative that we build societies that accommodate all in a manner that is sustainable and can inspire productivity.

> …growth potential exists regardless of whether that potential is nurtured or exploited remains yet to be evident.

I believe a lot of work is required in Nigeria to improve the overall well-being of the population. The issue of housing or affordability of supply is an important aspect of our society that requires a lot of attention and commitment from local, state, and federal institutions. However, growth potential exists regardless of whether that potential is nurtured or exploited remains yet to be evident.

Despite all the current challenges, the housing market holds the key to unlocking Nigeria's industrial capacity. As is evident already, many success stories (e.g. growing furniture industry) reveal how a growing middle-class, can change the landscape to one that inspires a generation to seek an identity in our unremitted potential.

www.ingramcontent.com/pod-product-compliance
Lightning Source LLC
Chambersburg PA
CBHW052330220526
45472CB00001B/351